SOUTHERN CALIFORNIA WINE COUNTRY
THROUGH TIME

The Vineyards and Wineries of Temecula

MARGE BITETTI

AMERICA
THROUGH TIME®
ADDING COLOR TO AMERICAN HISTORY

This book is dedicated to the numerous families and farm workers who helped develop the wine industry in Southern California; to my daughter, Danielle, for her assistance with this book; and to John Ortega for his unconditional support

America Through Time is an imprint of Fonthill Media LLC
www.through-time.com
office@through-time.com

Published by Arcadia Publishing by arrangement with Fonthill Media LLC
For all general information, please contact Arcadia Publishing:
Telephone: 843-853-2070
Fax: 843-853-0044
E-mail: sales@arcadiapublishing.com
For customer service and orders:
Toll-Free 1-888-313-2665

www.arcadiapublishing.com

First published 2019

Copyright © Marge Bitetti 2019

ISBN 978-1-63499-170-4

Typeset in 10pt on 13pt Mrs Eaves XL Serif Narrow
Printed and bound in England

CONTENTS

	Acknowledgments	5
	Introduction: Overview of Temecula	6
1	The Wineries	17
2	Akash Winery	19
3	Fazeli Cellars	22
4	Palumbo Family Vineyards & Winery	26
5	Cougar Vineyard & Winery	28
6	Oak Mountain Winery	39
7	South Coast Winery & Resort and Carter Estate Winery	41
8	Wilson Creek Winery	47
9	Baily Vineyard & Winery and Baily Estate Tasting Room	60
10	Wiens Family Cellars	68
11	Vitagliano Vineyards and Winery	76
12	Gershon Bachus Vintners	77
13	Vindemia Winery	78
14	Chapin Family Vineyards	81
15	Don Fernando Vineyard	84
16	Foot Path Winery	91
	Bibliography	95

Acknowledgments

Thank you to the Temecula History Museum and Temecula Wine Growers Association.

Working on this book has been an educational and memorable experience. Thanks are owed to so many people who helped make this book possible. I learned so much about the families who saw the possibilities and acted on their dreams to make Temecula a renowned wine producing region. The members of the family owned and operated wineries in the Temecula Valley have wine running through their veins. It is not about just serving the many customers, but more about making them part of the large extended wine lovers' family. The wine production is not just an industry, it is a way of life. It involves making friends with neighboring wineries and honoring them with the philosophy that when one succeeds, the entire Temecula wine region succeeds.

Special thanks to the following people who assisted greatly to make this book possible: Phil Baily, Cori Dehore, BJ Fazeli, Steven Galt, Beth Wiens Tichenor, and Mick Wilson.

Photo credits

Front cover
Top photo: Wilson Creek Winery (page 59)
Bottom photo: Fazeli Vineyard & Fazeli Cellars (page 24)

Back cover
Top photo: Cougar and Winery (page 33)
Bottom photo: Wilson Family, Wilson Creek Family Winery (page 55)

INTRODUCTION: OVERVIEW OF TEMECULA

History

The city of Temecula was established in 1859. It is in the extreme southwestern section of Riverside County and is 58 miles north of San Diego, 86 miles from Los Angeles and 49 miles south of San Bernardino County.

The name Temecula comes from the Luiseño Indian word *Temecunga—temet*—meaning "sun" and "-ngna" which means "place of." The Spanish settlers who came into the region translated it to mean, "Where the sun breaks through the mist."

The hillsides of Temecula were the home of Temecula Indians, the first residents of the area. Ancestors of Temecula Indians were here as early as AD 900. The Luiseno Indians still inhabited Temecula in the 1700s when the first Spanish padres arrived. The first known European man to set foot in this area was a Franciscan padre, Father Juan Norberto de Santiago, who arrived in the valley in 1797. The early vineyards in the region were planted by the Franciscans missionaries who planted the vines to make sacramental wine. At the end of the Spanish American War, the Treaty of Guadalupe Hidalgo in 1845 transferred the control of all of California to the United States. In 1875, the struggle for control of land between the settlers arriving from the east and the Europeans resulted in many of the Temecula Indians being forced from the area.

Over more than 200 years, the city of Temecula was settled in three different locations. First were the native Luiseno villages that were settled along Murrieta Creek. The second location of Temecula began in the nineteenth century to where the Redhawk Bridge crosses Temecula Creek. The third and present location of Temecula resulted from the train tracks that were laid by the Southern Pacific Railroad with tracks that went through Temecula Valley. The area of Temecula known as Old Town was the center of town.

Temecula became incorporated as a city in 1989. Today the population is just over 113,000.

The arch leading to Temecula's Old Town area has a flavor of the Old West.

Vineyards

The development of the region as a renowned wine producing area occurred centuries later. Temecula Valley received formal recognition as an American Viticultural Area in 1984, first as "Temecula AVA" with a subsequent name change to "Temecula Valley AVA" in 2004. Temecula Valley now boasts over forty licensed wineries, producing over 500,000 cases annually. The 50th Anniversary was celebrated in 2018.

The wineries of Temecula have a long history; however, the commercial wine industry in the region is still relatively new. A popular wine industry magazine recently listed Temecula as one of the top ten wine regions in the world that is worthy of visiting.

The city of Temecula has a unique character: the hills and valleys are lush and green and have rambling acres of vineyards. The downtown area of Temecula, referred to as Old Town, has remnants of the Old West. The is a collection of historic buildings, antiques stores, and restaurants. The wooden sidewalks resemble a scene from a Western movie.

Many of the wineries in Temecula Valley are family owned and operated. Visitors are greeted with warm hospitality, besides enjoying award winning wines, the atmosphere at all the wineries is friendly and welcoming. The region produces 500,000 cases of various wines produced in the valley.

Grape vines have been grown in the Temecula Valley since the mission day in the 1830s.

Front Street in Old Town looks like a setting from a Western movie.

The cactus that are planted in Temecula's Old Town are in contract to the green vineyard in the rolling hills.

The dreams of these pioneer families caused the wine industry to flourish in Temecula. Today, there are over forty licensed wineries in the Temecula Valley, many of them producing award winning wines annually. During the Prohibition of the 20s and 30s, the Temecula had several bootleggers and speakeasies. The first modern commercial vineyard was established in 1968.

In the 1800s, the Butterfield Overland Stage was contracted by the federal government to deliver mail and supplies to the West. The stage route followed the Southern Emigrant Trail. This trail passed through Temecula and brought thousands of setters west to California.

Above: The rolling hills of Temecula in winter with a dormant vineyard in the foreground.

Left: Butterfield Square in the heart of Temecula echoes the city's historic past.

The Butterfield Stage brought the mail to California from the East Coast.

A local artist depicted the early days of Temecula in this public art mural.

Today, one of the major streets in Temecula honors the Butterfield history.

This nostalgic mural in Old Town Temecula recalls when the Southern Pacific Railroad had a stop in Temecula, which ended in 1935.

Vail Ranch

In 1905, Walter Vail, who was an Arizona cattle baron, purchased land that had been settled 1867 by Louis Wolf, a German immigrant. He and his wife, Ramona, established a trading post near Temecula Creek. In 1905, after the death of the Wolfs, Walter Vail purchased the land that had belonged to the Wolfs along with other Ranchos, totaling 87,000 acres. The Vail Ranch became one of the largest cattle ranches in California, stretching from Camp Pendleton, near Oceanside in San Diego County, to Murrieta. Walter Vail was killed in a streetcar accident in Los Angeles in 1906, and his son, Mahlon, took over the management of the land. In 1964, Kaiser Aluminum and Macco Realty formed a partnership and purchased the Vail Ranch land. This purchase led wine production in the valley. Plans are in progress for the restoration of the Vail Ranch buildings.

Highway 395

The increased population and the development of the automobile created a need for paved roads. Route 395, which was commissioned in 1926, was built to provide travel between San Diego and the State of Washington. The road passed through Temecula, connecting Riverside and San Bernardino Counties with northern cities, and stretched for 557 miles.

In between the vineyards, there are still wide stretches of bare land like the days when the Vail Ranch was in full operation.

A Hint of Hollywood in Temecula

It was rumored that in the 1920s Temecula was the playground for Hollywood celebrities, and that the hills of Temecula were home to moonshining; however, there is not substantial proof for either. However, it is fact that well-known mystery writer Erle Stanley Gardner made his home in Temecula at Rancho del Paisano from 1937 until his death in 1970. He was a prolific writer and the author of over ninety best sellers, best known as the author the *Perry Mason Mysteries*, which were produced into 271 episodes for television during the 1950s. Cable television channels occasionally still air old *Perry Mason* re-runs. The Temecula History Museum has a tribute to Gardner, including a recreation of his office. Temecula had been the location for several movies and television shows, including: 1996 movie *Weekend in the Country*; 2009 movie *The Goods: Live Hard, Sell Hard*; and the final episode of *Star Trek: The Next Generation*.

Festivals

In 1983, Walt Darren, a commercial airline pilot, and Evelyn Harker, an avid balloonist, organized the first Temecula Balloon Festival, originally called Rancho California Balloon and Wine Festival. The first festival was funded by seed money provided by Kaiser Development Company. The event is usually set in May or June and attracts thousands of visitors. Numerous name bands have performed at the festival in the past including: The Beach Boys, Blake Shelton, Kenny Loggins, Sugar Ray, Collective Soul, Gin Blossoms, James Otto, Chuck Wicks, and Peter Frampton. 2019 was the thirty-sixth year that the Balloon Festival has attracted visitors to Temecula Valley. It is held above Lake Skinner. It is a colorful sight to view so many hot air balloons in flight over the valley. The festival also includes wine tasting, foods, and arts and crafts.

Other festivals in Temecula: Temecula Bluegrass Festival, Temecula Valley International Film and Music Festival, Temecula Valley International Jazz Festival, Temecula Street Painting Festival, and the Temecula Greek Festival.

Climate

Temecula Valley welcomes more than two million visitors each year. The casual, picturesque Temecula Valley is a year-round getaway and vacation destination located sixty minutes from San Diego, Orange County, and Palm Springs, and ninety minutes from Los Angeles and Hollywood. A memorable day trip or weekend getaway, Temecula is the jewel of the Inland Empire, offering a wide choice of five-star resort accommodations and restaurants, as well as an abundance of leisure activities that range from balloon tours over the valley to horseback riding. Surrounding the Temecula Valley Wine Country are the Palomar Mountains, the Rainbow Gap, and Santa Margarita Gap. Popular boutique destination includes the Temecula Valley A.V.A. (American Viticulture Area) as well as Downtown Old Town Temecula, Pechanga Resort & Casino, and the De Portola Wine Trail. The climate is ideal for wine production and is like the noted regions of Bordeaux, Burgundy, and Loire Valley in France, and the Moselle Valley and Rhine Region in German. It is particularly suited for growing Italian, Spanish, and French varieties of grapes such as: Sangiovese, Syrah, and Zinfandel. Temecula Valley is at an elevation of 1,500 feet at a Latitude of 33, which is like Napa Valley in Northern California. The region has a Mediterranean climate characterized by warm, dry summers, cool nights, and mild winters.

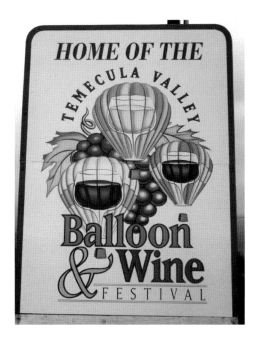

Right: Temecula Balloon Festival has been a favorite summer event in Temecula for the past thirty-six years.

Below: The Mediterranean climate in Temecula is the idea climate for growing excellent grapes for wine production.

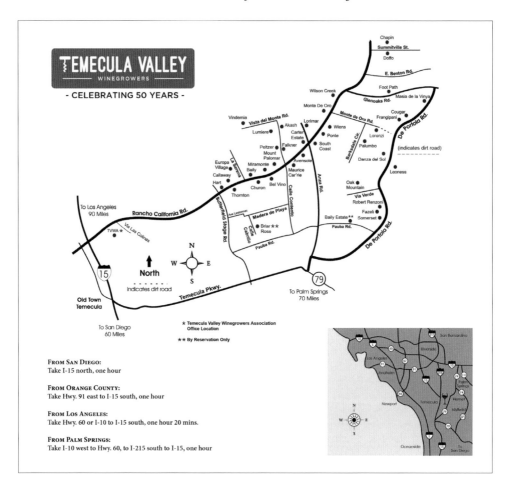

Above: Map of Temecula Wine Country. [*Courtesy of Temecula Valley Wine Growers Association*]

Left: These directional signs are posted throughout the Temecula Valley to direct visitors to the wineries.

1

THE WINERIES

Listing of area wineries by street

Rancho California Road
Avensole
Bel Vino
Chapin
Carter Estate Winery & Resort
Callaway Vineyard & Winery
Maurice Car'rie Vineyard & Winery
Miramont Winery
Monte De Oro Winery
Mount Palomar Winery
Ponte Winery
South Coast Winery
Thornton Winery
Wilson Creek Winery

De Portola Road
Cougar Winery
Danza Del Sol Winery
Fazeli Cellars
Frangipani Estate Winery
Gershon Bachus Vintners
Leoness Cellars
Robert Renzoni Vineyards

Via Verde
Oak Mountain Winery

Via Del Ponte
Wiens Family Cellars

Vista Del Monte
Vindemia Vineyards & Estate Winery

Glen Oaks Road
Foot Path winery

Monte de Oro Road
Lorenzi Estate Vineyard & Winery

Avenida Biona
Hart

Anza Road
Lorimar Vineyards & Winery

La Serena
Europa Village

Pauba Road
Baily Estate Tasting Room

Calle Contento
Falkner Winery
Lumiere Winery
Peltzer Family Cellars

Barksdale Circle
Palumbo Family Vineyards & Winery

Calle Cabrillo
Briar Rose Winery

Camino Arroyo Seco
Masia De La Vinya Winery

Summitville
Doffo Winery

Early Wine Operations

The beginnings of Temecula turning into a commercial wine region started in the 1960s. John Moramarco, who was from a winegrowing family in Cucamonga, visited Temecula with Philo Biane, the owner of Brookside Winery, which was in Guasti. Their visit was to determine the possible expansion of Brookside winery in the Temecula Valley. Brookside planted 1,000 acres.

In 1969 Golf Pro Ely Callaway and John Poole purchased several acres and hired viticulturist, John Moramarco, who believed that the area was ideal for growing premium wine grapes. Moramarco, supervised the planting and operations of the fledgling vineyard. In 1978, Brookside sold the company's vineyards and winery operations.

Temecula Wine Industry: 1970s to Present

In 1971, Brookside Winery planted on more than 400 acres. Another pioneer in the Temecula wine industry was Phil Baily.

In 1975, John Poole opened Mount Palomar Winery; this was the first winery in the valley to focus on visitors. In 1978, the valley pioneer wine growers, Vincenzo and Audrey Cilurzo, together with Dr. John Piconi, opened the Cilurzo-Piconi Winery, which is now Bella Vista Winery.

Signpost are throughout Temecula Valley. The T in the word Temecula is a corkscrew.

2

AKASH WINERY

Akash Winery & Vineyard is owned and operated by father and son, Ray and Akash Patel. With a lifelong dream of having their own winery, Ray and Akash invested in 20 acres of land in the beautiful Temecula Valley Wine country in 2010.

The story of the winery begins at the vineyard, located in the heart of Temecula's wine country, on Calle Contento. The vineyard stretches across the parcel where the Patel's, winemaker Renato Sais, and the winery staff give the vines the upmost care all year long. Working together, learning and understanding viniculture, curating the perfect grape and vine, and learning the wine business have become a huge passion for the duo. 100% estate grown, Akash wines are developed with passion and sophistication. The wines showcase familiar varietals in contemporary, eye-catching packaging. The Akash Winery & Vineyard tasting room is fairly new and has a charming atmosphere accented by large metal wine tanks and assorted furniture. Private tastings are also available by reservation. The Patels also hope to open a resort, spa, venue, and bed & breakfast in the coming years.

The people involved with Akash Winery includes Akash Patel, Nalini Patel, Renato Sais, Sharon Cannon, and Darius Guerrero. Akash Winery grows the following varieties of grapes at the vineyard: sauvignon blanc, zinfandel, cabernet sauvignon, petite Syrah, and cabernet Franc. Akash Winery produces sauvignon blanc, rosé, zinfandel, cabernet sauvignon, petite Syrah, and Three's Company, which is a blend of zinfandel, cabernet, and petite Syrah.

Work in the vineyard at Akash Winery. [*Courtesy of Akash Winery*]

Ray and Akash Patel looking over the grapes in their vineyard. [*Courtesy of Akash Winery*]

Construction continues at Akash Vineyard. [*Courtesy of Akash Winery*]

Akash Vineyard. [*Courtesy of Akash Winery*]

3

Fazeli Cellars

Fazeli Cellars (TM) is the trademark of Fazeli Vineyards LLC.

Fazeli Winery is the only Southern California Persian heritage winery. Owner Bizhan "BJ" Fazeli had a desire to share the rich history of wine that is tied to the Persian culture. A family drive to Temecula in 2001 was life changing because it was that trip that inspired BJ Fazeli to build his winery in Temecula. He selected shiraz as the benchmark varietal for his winery. Shiraz wine has is integral to Persian culture. Iranians have enjoyed this wine for centuries it was evident in Persian mythology, poetry, and art. The winery has grown over the years to include facilities for weddings and banquets, and Baba Joon's kitchen, which provides a fusion of Persia and contemporary California dishes. It is open daily. Fazeli Cellars also offers live music on the weekends. What started out as the owner's passion to produce fine wine has blossomed. The beautiful facility, friendly staff and the warm personality of Fazeli's owner helped to made Fazeli Cellars a delightful location to visit.

The red wines at Fazeli Cellars are aged to perfection in French, Hungarian, and American barrels before being bottled. The 10-12,000 cases of annual production are released to consistent demand. Careful consideration was also made when it came to select the unique names of the wines—each of which have a meaningful connection to Fazeli's Persian heritage.

Fazeli Cellars' popular Seasons Collection celebrates Narooz, named after the spring equinox, that coincides with the start of the Persian New Year. The varietals—Viognier and Muscat canelli—are refreshing white wines with floral aromas. Embrace the Chaos is a collection of wines that includes Pandemonium—a rich blend of five difference varietal—and Mayhem, a savory blend of cinsault and mourvedre. For wine that's sheer poetry, The Heritage Collection pays homage to four noble Persian poets. Among the most popular of the Fazeli wines, the collection consists of cabernet sauvignon, cabernet Franc, petite Syrah, and shiraz.

Early days of the major construction at Fazeli Cellars. [*Courtesy of Fazeli Cellars*]

Construction of the main facility at Fazeli Cellars. A day trip in 2001 by the Fazeli Family resulted in the successful Fazeli Cellars. [*Courtesy of Fazeli Cellars*]

Fazeli Main facility before completion. [*Courtesy of Fazeli Cellars*]

The Fazeli Vineyard. What started out as the owner's passion to produce fine wine has blossomed. [*Courtesy of Fazeli Cellars*]

The design of the Fazeli main building honors Persian traditions. [*Courtesy of Fazeli Cellars*]

The buildings at Fazeli blend to form a geometric and architectural showplace. [*Courtesy of Fazeli Cellars*]

The Moorish architecture and ambiance of the winery honors ancient Persian traditions, while paying tribute to the contemporary character of California as is reflected on the back label of all their wines "Ancient traditions of Persia rooted in the modern expression of California."

PALUMBO FAMILY VINEYARDS & WINERY

Nicholas Palumbo, passionate Viticulturist and budding Oenologist, believes in producing only what he grows himself. "I believe there is only two basic ingredients in making fine wines, the fruit itself and the barrels it ages in". With one foot in modern techniques and the other foot firmly planted in tradition, the wines produced possess a depth and elegance that is becoming harder to find in California wines.

The Palumbo's purchased the property in 1998 and opened the tasting room in November of 2002. They have been in operation for seventeen years. Palumbo Winery is also a California Certified Sustainable Winery and Vineyards. They practice sustainability not only in how they run their business buy how they farm and even how they raise their family. Cindy Palumbo is heavily involved in raising food for her family's consumption. Nick Palumbo is an avid fisherman and catches whatever Cindy doesn't raise. Cindy currently sits on the Board of Directors for the 46th District Agricultural Association for the State of California

Along with his wife, Cindy, and their four children, Reed, Ryan, Sophia and Dominick, the Palumbo's believe that the vineyards come first. They have a total of twenty-three acres, thirteen devoted to the winery. They have planted cabernet sauvignon, cabernet franc, merlot and sangiovese varietals. A block of viognier and Syrah was planted on neighboring properties to round out the line of wines available. The Palumbo's purchased a ten-acre parcel out in the hills of DeLuz where they also planted tannat, Syrah and grenache.

Specializing in full-bodied reds, the estate-grown and produced offerings include both single variety bottling's as well as a few special blends, like the very popular Meritage called "Tre Fratelli." Other blends like the shiraz/cabernet sauvignon help round out the wine list and showcase the versatility and depth of quality that the Palumbo wines are known for.

The Palumbo Family from left to right, Kori, Ryan, Dominick (front), Cindy, Nick, Sophia, Reed. [*Courtesy Palumbo Family Vineyards*]

Nick and Cindy Palumbo and their children daily work at the winery. [*Courtesy Palumbo Family Vineyards*]

COUGAR VINEYARD & WINERY

Rick and Jennifer Buffington started making wine in Texas more than twenty-five years ago. Making good wine in an 85-degree room, Jennifer commented: "Yes, the air conditioner was on. "It wasn't easy."

Even though the conditions weren't optimum for wine making, they managed to pull off some great wine. At the time, they bottled under the Ironstone Trail Winery label.

Later, Rick and Jennifer traded in the blistering Texas heat for the cool Seattle weather. They began making wine from grapes obtained from Eastern Washington. While living in Seattle, Rick and Jennifer frequently traveled to Buhl, Idaho, to visit a friend and fellow winemaker. During one trip, they helped their friend plant an acre of Chardonnay grapes. It was then that Rick and Jennifer started thinking about a vineyard of their own.

Rick and Jennifer had to wait, however, since they couldn't grow anything around their property that was snail- and slug-proof. Meanwhile, they continued to make wine, producing some very good reds and finally some whites to be proud of, placing third for their Semillon in the 1998 Washington State Fair. They bottled under the Cougar Mountain Winery label, named for the mountain located east of Seattle.

Finally, Rick and Jennifer moved to Fallbrook, California, where they planted a vineyard on their home property. Over seven years they planted 1,000 vines, including sangiovese, montepulciano, Malbec, cabernet sauvignon, and Syrah. Rick and Jennifer were active members of the San Diego Amateur Winemaking Society, from which they learned techniques for growing the best grapes and making the highest quality wine.

The winery property is more than ten gross acres. Cougar farms an additional twenty acres, including La Vigna a Destra, the winemakers' home in Fallbrook and other property in Temecula wine country.

Rick and Jennifer Buffington when they broke ground at Cougar Winery. [*Courtesy Cougar Vineyard & Winery*]

Construction of facility Cougar Vineyard & Winery. [*Courtesy Cougar Vineyard & Winery*]

The couple was not able to grow anything while they were in Washington. [*Courtesy Cougar Vineyard & Winery*]

With construction completed, Jennifer and Rick opened the doors to Cougar Winery to the public after crush in 2006. [*Courtesy Cougar Vineyard & Winery*]

Above: Rick & Jennifer won a gold medal in the Orange County Fair for Sauvignon Blanc. During this time, the Cougar Vineyard & Winery label was born. [*Courtesy Cougar Vineyard & Winery*]

Right: In 2005, Rick and Jennifer purchased the winery property on De Portola Road in Temecula and settled on Italian varietals after discovering that the territory was particularly suitable to grapes grown in the Mediterranean country. [*Courtesy Cougar Vineyard & Winery*]

Wine Cask Cougar Vineyards & Winery produces 8,500 cases of wine annually and continues to increase production each year. [*Courtesy Cougar Vineyard & Winery*]

Rick and Jennifer Buffington started making wine in Texas more than twenty-five years ago. It was difficult making wine in an 85-degree room, but they succeeded. [*Courtesy Cougar Vineyard & Winery*]

Cozy tables in the tasting area provide guest with an opportunity to relax and enjoy the wine and the surroundings. [*Courtesy Cougar Vineyard & Winery*]

Cougar specializes in Italian red, white, and sparkling wines, including peach and strawberry sangrias. A few of the popular wines that are produced at Cougar include:

2016 Coda di Volpe
Also known as "Fox Tail," Coda di Volpe is a rare find in the Temecula Valley, let alone North America. It is typically grown in Naples, which is part of the Campania region of Italy. This crisp light acidic white wine has notes of melon. Cougar successfully petitioned the Alcohol and Tobacco Tax and Trade Bureau (TTB) to recognize the grape as a varietal in the United States.

2017 Estate Falanghina
A take on an ancient grape from Campania, Italy, this grape variety does very well in the warm Temecula climate. Crisp Anjou and Asian pears show on the nose along with Gala apple and white flowers. Sharp citrus appears on the palate, with a hint of lime and pink grapefruit.

2015 Estate Primitivo
100% varietal wine originating from the Apulia region of Italy. This wine possesses a nice dark fruit and spicy nose which complements the smooth mouth feel and soft lingering finish.

Left: Custom chairs on the patio overlooking De Portola Road, a popular draw for Cougar's visitors. Each chair is as one-of-a-kind as the maker, who was a Cougar employee and has since passed away. The first chairs were made in 2008 and over the next three years, the number grew to twelve chairs total. [*Courtesy Cougar Vineyard & Winery*]

Below: All wines are produced in house and most are made with estate-grown grapes. [*Courtesy Cougar Vineyard & Winery*]

Right: Vermentino harvest, this grape produces a light-bodied white wine that is complex in taste and similar style to Sauvignon Blanc. [*Courtesy Cougar Vineyard & Winery*]

Below: Aerial view of Cougar Vineyard and Winery. [*Courtesy Cougar Vineyard & Winery*]

2014 Estate Lambrusca di Alessandria

Lambrusca di Alessandria is a rare grape originally from the Piedmont region of Italy. Dark with aromas of black cherries and anise and a smooth finish. Cougar successfully petitioned the TTB to recognize the grape as a varietal in the United States.

2014 Estate Negroamaro

Another rare grape from the Puglia region. Rich with spicy notes, red fruit, coffee, and blackberry. Pairs great with spicy food.

2017 Brachetto Bubbly

Made with their Estate Brachetto and a splash of their Estate Prosecco. Brachetto is mainly grown in the Piedmonte region of northwest Italy. Cougar petitioned and got the grape recognized as a varietal in the United States.

Awards

In 2018, *Inland Empire Magazine* honored Cougar with the following wine tasting awards: Gold for 2014 Lambrusca di Alessandria, Gold for 2014 Negroamaro, and Silver for 2016 Vermentino. Every year since 2016, the winery hosts "Cougar Meets Italy," a blind tasting competition in which wine industry professionals and wine club members, customers, family and friends judge a selection of Cougar wines against their Italian counterparts. This year, the experts selected two out of five of Cougar's wines, while the People's Choice Award went to three of Cougar's five wines. Cougar Meets Italy is inspired by *Bottle Shock*, the movie based on the famous 1976 Judgment of Paris that put California wine on the map. In 2005, Rick and Jennifer purchased the winery property on De Portola Road in Temecula and settled on Italian varietals after discovering that the terrain was particularly suitable to grapes grown in the Mediterranean country.

They initially planted sangiovese, aglianico, montepulciano, and vermentino grapes. Later, they added falanghina, canaiolo Nero, Ciliegiolo, Glera (formerly known as Prosecco), and Piedirosso. Next door, on the property known as "La Vigna a Destra," they planted Primitivo, Arneis, malvasia bianca, pinot grigio, sagrantino, Nero d' Avola, Piedirosso, and Lambrusca di Alessandria. Rick and Jennifer opened their doors for wine tasting to the public after the 2006 crush.

Cougar Vineyard and Winery during the Temecula Balloon Festival. [*Courtesy Cougar Vineyard & Winery*]

Veraison grapes show the change of color of the grape berries as the berries ripen. [*Courtesy Cougar Vineyard & Winery*]

Above: Rick Buffington takes a break after a grape harvest. [*Courtesy Cougar Vineyard & Winery*]

Left: A cheerful welcome sign greets visitors to Cougar Winery. [*Courtesy Cougar Vineyard & Winery*]

6

OAK MOUNTAIN WINERY

Steve and Valerie Andrews are the owners of Oak Mountain Winery and Temecula Hills Winery in Temecula, California. In 1996, Valerie met her future husband and business partner, Steve Andrews, who owned a successful towing business at the time. They were married in 1999 and moved to a 14-acre ranch just on the edge of Temecula's wine country, where they built Temecula Hills Winery and the Oak Mountain brand from scratch. The vines were planted in 2000 by Valerie, Steve, and their children personally, so the wines are the result of their labor of love.

Now in the second decade of their wine careers, the Andrews are deeply loved by the community and consumers and admired and respected by their colleagues. Valerie balances her time running the day-to-day business operations at both wineries, as well as serving on the board for the De Portola Wine Trail. Steve manages the vineyards, bottling, and all winemaking duties.

Steve and Valerie are devoted to their family and the community. They have succeeded in raising a son and two daughters as well as four grandchildren, while successfully managing their careers. Steve and Valerie have reputations for being innovative thinkers, driven, creative, confidant, and generous. Their belief is "being a member of the community means contributing to the community."

In 1999, The Andrews founded Cause for Paws, a 501(c)(3) nonprofit organization whose mission is assisting animals with diabetes and helping senior citizens with companion pets. Cause for Paws Inc. helps low income pet owners pay for 100% of their medical needs. The Andrews also inspired their son and his wife, who also work at the family winery, to help animals in need. Animal Town Sanctuary, a senior dog sanctuary, was inspired by Andrews' kindness towards animals. Dog labeled wines and hand-crafted cork tiaras can be found at Oak Mountain Winery, with proceeds going to help local animals in need. Oak Mountain is the site of numerous dog events and charity fundraisers throughout the year. The winery encourages their customers to bring their well-mannered dogs with them to the winery to enjoy the day.

Oak Mountain Winery is a fun, family owned winery that is located on the De Portola Wine Trail, in Temecula's Wine Country. Home to Southern California's only mined wine caves, Oak Mountain offers tours and tastings with knowledgeable and friendly staff. Oak Mountain is renowned for their famous Raspberry and Strawberry Champagnes as well as over thirty award winning wines. Guests can dine underground at Oak Mountain's Cave Café. Wedding and special events are also popular at the winery. The climate-controlled pavilion at the winery overlooks the lush view of Temecula Valley. Oak Mountain Winery provides free wi-fi and live music every Sunday.

The Barrel Room at Oak Mountain Winery. [*Courtesy Oak Mountain Winery*]

One couple who celebrated their wedding at Oak Mountain decided to include an elephant in the celebration. [*Courtesy Oak Mountain Winery*]

7

SOUTH COAST WINERY & RESORT AND CARTER ESTATE WINERY

People who are familiar with the Temecula Valley in Southern California may also be familiar with the 63-acre South Coast Winery Resort & Spa, since it has broken records in both domestic and international competitions over the years, accumulating over 5,000 awards and medals, including becoming the only winery to be the four-time winner of the prestigious California State Winery of the Year in 2016 from the California State Fair Commercial Wine Competition. Yet few are aware of its founder, Jim Carter, who built this region's shining star, South Coast Winery Resort & Spa.

Born and raised in Ohio, Carter, like most kids, loved digging in the dirt. By age sixteen, he landed a job with a framer and began his career as a builder. Carter's love for building brought him to California at the age of eighteen, and upon making that move, he was named the "youngest carpenter journeyman to ever enter into the union."

Carter's love for the "craft of building"—from digging up the earth and laying the foundation to putting on the roof and landscaping, led him to start several businesses throughout the ensuing years, and in one year, he built over 2,500 homes.

Projects got bigger and he kept building and reinvesting into more. Carter expanded his portfolio to not only include master home developments but also apartment complexes, shopping centers, a 250-acre tree farm, a 400-acre parcel of land, a bank, and ultimately a successful savings and loan just before the savings and loan disaster of the 90s—when he learned an important lesson in cash flow.

For the next ten years, Carter struggled dangerously close to losing the home in which he and his wife raised their children. He aggressively sold his assets and reduced his workforce from 500+ down to fifty employees, as banks continued to turn their backs on him.

In 1995, while watching the movie *A Walk in the Clouds*, he experienced a life-changing epiphany, connecting with the movie's storyline of a thriving vineyard in a beautiful mountain valley that closely resembled the 400-acre parcel of land he had hung onto throughout those troubling years, which sits in the valley of the Santa Rosa Plateau Palomar Mountain Range. With the assistance of his children and the gardeners from his apartment complexes, along with the quarters he collected from the laundry facilities of those complexes, Carter planted a vineyard, known today as Wild Horse Peak Mountain Vineyards.

Following the tumultuous years of struggling with financial lending institutions, Carter was now building a world-class vineyard. Contracts came from other wineries to purchase fruit from Carter's Southern California vineyards, and life settled into a pattern.

South Coast Winery was the dream of founder Jim Carter. This photo shows the early stages of the winery. [*Courtesy of South Coast Winery*]

Building progress of South Coast Winery. The facility now includes a spa, hotel, and premiere restaurant. [Courtesy of South Coast Winery]

South Coast Winery Resort & Spa features 30,000 square feet of meeting space and a variety of outdoor venues with full catering service. Ideal for weddings, business conferences, and other noteworthy occasions. [*Courtesy of South Coast Winery*]

Progress on the building of South Coast Winery. [*Courtesy of South Coast Winery*]

In 1995, with the assistance of his children, the gardeners from his apartment complexes, along with the quarters he collected from the laundry facilities of those complexes, Carter planted a vineyard, known today as Wild Horse Peak Mountain Vineyards. [*Courtesy of South Coast Winery*]

Early landscaping at South Coast Winery. [*Courtesy of South Coast Winery*]

When one of his largest winery clients decided to no longer purchase Wild Horse Peak Mountain Vineyard fruit, the idea of Temecula Valley's first winery resort was birthed. Shortly thereafter, Carter brought in the finest winemakers, purchased Rolling Hills Vineyard and South Coast Vineyard in the Temecula appellation, and began building the area's very first full-service winery resort. In late 2015, after years of planning and hard work, the Valley welcomed Carter's newest addition of premier resort wineries and, in honoring his family's traditions and values, named it Carter Estate Winery and Resort.

Pulling into the olive-tree-lined driveway, guests have the opportunity to stop in the winery's tasting room to experience Carter Estate's menu of award-winning wines and estate grown olive oils or continue on through the driveway into a gated area, reserved exclusively for overnight guests, adorned with seventy-eight spacious bungalows touting expansive vineyard vistas, a pool, and breathtaking outdoor dining venue serving breakfast, lunch, and dinner.

Today, Carter continues to raise the bar. South Coast Winery Resort & Spa and Carter Estate Winery and Resort are truly "diamonds of the Temecula Valley," producing a broad portfolio of award-winning wines and five-star hospitality.

Carter found himself testing the soils, the water, lighting and temperatures on the 400-acre parcel of land and determined the conditions ideal for growing outstanding varietals of grapes. [*Courtesy of South Coast Winery*]

In 2015, Carter Estate Winery and Resort opened. [*Courtesy of South Coast Winery*]

Situated on 112-acres, Carter Estate Winery and Resort is positioned to become one of the state's preeminent méthode champenoise sparkling wine producers. [*Courtesy of South Coast Winery*]

8

WILSON CREEK WINERY

The Wilson family loved to entertain and brought their Midwestern hospitality with them. Gerry was a financial advisor, while Rosie was a former TV cooking show host. Family and work placed at the top of the list of their priorities.

In 1996, the Wilson family decided to create a small winery in Temecula. They sold their home in South Pasadena and, by the next year, three of their children and their spouses picked up from where they were living to move to Temecula as well.

The warm friendly hospitality found at Wilson Creek Winery is like the atmosphere that the family created for friends and neighbors in their home.

In the mid-1990s, the family found a winery that was for sale in Temecula. They purchased twenty acres and started construction. The official opening of Wilson Creek Winery was in October 2000.

Wilson Creek was the fifteenth winery to open in the Temecula Valley. Mick Wilson said, "We made wine FUN."

The family's background in making people feel welcome carried over to the winery, tasting room, wine club, and special events. By the end of the fifth year of operation, the winery produced 5,000 cases of wine. Most recently the winery produced 100,000 cases of wine. Today, they own ninety acres and sell over 75,000 cases of wine each year. Each weekend, the winery welcomes more than 1,500 visitors.

Their winery hosts multiple charity events each year that bring in hundreds of thousands of dollars, and the Temecula Valley Chamber of Commerce named them Gold Business of the Year four times. This family enterprise started with a dream, before it grew into the successful commercial entity it has become since the tasting room opened in 2000.

One of the popular items at Wilson Creek is the almond Champagne along with a total of six popular sparkling wines. The Wilson Family has created a location where people want to relax and spend time. The vision and dream of a successful winery that inspired the senior members of the family has successfully been passed on the younger generations.

Today, they own ninety acres and sell over 75,000 cases of wine each year. Each weekend, the winery welcomes more than 1,500 visitors. Their winery hosts multiple charity events each year that bring in hundreds of thousands of dollars for the charities. This family enterprise started with a dream, before it grew into the successful commercial entity it has become since the tasting room opened in 2000.

Wilson Creek was the fifteenth winery to open in Temecula Valley. Like many of the wineries in the Temecula Valley, Wilson Creek is a family owned and operated business. [*Courtesy of the Wilson Family*]

The success of Wilson Creek Winery started with the vision of Gerry and Rosie Wilson. [*Courtesy of the Wilson Family*]

Bill Wilson on the roof during the construction of the winery. [*Courtesy of the Wilson Family*]

Temporary trailer beside building with metal frame construction. [*Courtesy of the Wilson Family*]

The Wilson Family during the winery's early years. The enduring success of Wilson Creek still is founded upon the love and commitment of the Wilson family members. [*Courtesy of the Wilson Family*]

Rosie Wilson working in one of the Wilson Creek lower garden areas. [*Courtesy of the Wilson Family*]

One of the family dogs keeping an eye on Rosie while she is working. [*Courtesy of the Wilson Family*]

Mick Wilson working in the vineyard. Wilson Creek was the fifteenth winery to open in the Temecula Valley. Mick Wilson said, "We made wine FUN." [*Courtesy of the Wilson Family*]

Bill Wilson working with the grape crush. [*Courtesy of the Wilson Family*]

Even the young family members help. Cambria helping with the crush. [*Courtesy of the Wilson Family*]

Wilson's family dogs, Taffy and Merlot, overseeing the grape crush. [*Courtesy of the Wilson Family*]

Members of the Wilson Family sample juice after the crush. [*Courtesy of the Wilson Family*]

One of the buildings at Wilson Creek. [*Courtesy of the Wilson Family*]

Grape vines cover the archway into one of the vineyards. [*Courtesy of the Wilson Family*]

The winery provides beautiful surroundings for weddings. [*Courtesy of the Wilson Family*]

The Wilson Family Winery is a family business. [*Courtesy of the Wilson Family*]

Grape vines in the Wilson Creek vineyard. [*Courtesy of the Wilson Family*]

Wine club members point to the photo wall. [*Courtesy of the Wilson Family*]

Invitation to join the Wilson Family wine Club. [*Courtesy of the Wilson Family*]

Wilson Creek Winery was named Gold Business of the year four times by the Temecula Valley Chamber of Commerce, the Wilson Family joined to celebrate this award.

The Wilson Creek Hot Air Balloon Floats above the Wilson Creek Winery during the annual Temecula Valley Balloon & Wine Festival.

9

BAILY VINEYARD & WINERY AND BAILY ESTATE TASTING ROOM

Like many of the wineries in the Temecula Valley, Baily Vineyard and Winery is family owned. Phil and Carol Baily moved with their two sons from the Los Angeles area to Temecula in 1981.

The couple were wine enthusiasts and had also done a little home winemaking. In 1982, the Bailys planted their first acre of grapes on Mother's Day. They soon began taking classes in viticulture and enology.

The vineyard expanded in 1983, it now comprises five and one-half acres, all planted in the Riesling variety. The soil is decomposed granite, and the southeast facing hillside site creates an early ripening environment which produces grapes of high natural acidity. The grapes have the classic apricot flavor prized in Riesling.

Through the years, the first acre expanded to twenty-seven acres and the building of a state-of-the-art production facility, a visitor center, tasting room, and Carol's restaurant.

The Bailys also open a tasting room on Pauba Road for library wines (aged, older premium reds). Phil is noted in the region for his first-hand knowledge of the history, geography, and development of the Temecula Valley as a well-recognized distinguished wine maker, and he has often given presentations to share his vast knowledge.

Over the years, the Bailys expanded their holdings, and in 1990 purchased one of Temecula's original vineyards, a twenty-acre parcel which was planted in 1968. In 1992, they opened Baily Wine Country Café located in Old Town Temecula and owned by son Chris and daughter-in-law Kim. In 1998, they opened their tasting room and restaurant, Carol's, on Rancho California Road, and in 2001 built a new, larger production facility at the site of the original winery on Pauba Road.

Exterior of the Baily Winery celebrating thirty years in Temecula Valley.

Phil and Carol Baily in the early years of the winery and vineyard.

Grapes vines at Baily Vineyard in the dormant winter season.

There are vast open spaces in the wine country near the Baily vineyard.

Berenda Vineyard

Planted primarily with Bordeaux varieties, cabernet sauvignon (five-and-one-half acres), cabernet franc (two acres), merlot (two acres), sauvignon blanc (two acres), and semillon (one acre), this vineyard was planted in 1968 and purchased by the Bailys in 1994. In 2005, one-and-one-half acres of Malbec and two-and-one-half acres of sangiovese were planted. While still classed as relatively poor soil, it tends to be somewhat richer than Mother's Vineyard, and especially suitable for these varieties.

The menu at Carol's Restaurant features a variety of beautiful entrée salads, appetizers, sandwiches, fresh fish, steak, and pasta dishes. If you enjoy a good Reuben sandwich, this is the place for you. Baily wines are available by the glass and bottle, as well as other wines. A wide selection of micro brewed beers and a local microbrew on tap are offered for the beer aficionado. Carol's also has a Private Dining Room available for parties where a buffet lunch or dinner is served for groups of twenty-four to forty-eight.

Baily wines are known for their smoothness and expressive varietal character, the result of spending thirty months in barrel, twelve to eighteen months longer than normal industry practice. And making wines from the same vineyards for over twenty years assures a consistency that few wineries in the region can match.

Now, with twenty-seven acres of grapes, a state-of-the-art production facility, a comfortable visitor center with tasting room and restaurant on the main road in wine country, and most recently, an exclusive appointment-only tasting room at the production facility, the Baily's have created the place where wine and food enthusiasts can taste the best the Temecula Valley has to offer.

La Serena Vineyard

Comprised of one-and-one-half acres of cabernet sauvignon and one acre of sauvignon blanc, these grapevines are the ones you see at the visitor center. Grown on sandy/clay soil, they produce wines with exceptionally fruity varietal aromas.

Carol Baily is featured in a news article.

The tasting room on Pauba Road is known for the liberty red wines and is in the middle of wide-open spaces.

Meritage is the flagship wine at Baily's. Meritage is a blend of Cabernet Sauvignon, Cabernet Franc, Malbec and Merlot, all grown at the Estate Vineyard on Berenda Road.

Right: In 1998 the Baily's opened their tasting room and Carol's Restaurant on Rancho California Road.

Below: Carol pouring wine in the early years of the winery.

New Baily Winery pour

CAROL BAILY POURS a glass of Cabernet Sauvignon Nouveau for two winery guests Saturday.

Above left: Carol in an early news story demonstrates a recipe for duck and pepper salad.

Above right: A newspaper article celebrates the Baily's Cabernet Nouveau.

Women winos

A behind-the-scenes look at the ladies whose passion is growing grapes

omen winos. There are no statistics available, but it's safe to say that not all of them reside on Skid Row in downtown Los Angeles.

In fact, a good number of them reside in Temecula Valley. They're the ones notorious for making the wine, not for drinking it.

Matter of fact, 50 percent of the 75 full time Callaway Vineyard & Winery employees are women. The founder of Callaway, Eli Callaway, once said that the winery business needed to attract buyers, he hired the first lady wine salesperson. Today all but one of the salespeople at Callaway are women. In northern California a woman also does the selling the Temecula Valley winery.

ly in the vineyard, which covers 320 and in the cellar do you find men. It comes time to bottling the finished the staff consists of 50 percent 50 percent women.

rding to Betz Collins, director of ty communications, most of their ir guides are women. Females in inary department also outnumber

Callaway is one of many wineries in Temecula Valley. Today there are more than 3,000 acres of vineyards in the region and more than eight wineries.

They are located just east of Interstate 15 on a 20 mile loop road that winds through lush, green vineyards and groves, horse farms and rolling, golden hills.

Experiments in wine making began in southern California in the 1960s when the University of California Davis experimented with several premium varieties in the warm south and proved that the particular micro-climate and granite-type soil of the Temecula hills were

well-suited for a handful of vinifera cultivars of merit.

The growing season, though originally classified as Region III or IV by the Davis heat summation formula, actually runs nearly 10 degrees cooler because of marine breezes that penetrate the valley through Rainbow Gap. The pacific breezes are drawn from the ocean only 25 miles to the west and effectively produce a growing season more similar to a Region II or warm Region I.

In 1968 the Cilurzo family of Temecula Valley became the first of the new pioneers of southern California wine grape

growers. They planted their Chen and Petite Sirah vines on the old Cattle Ranch. They were greeted ranches and horse farms, avoca and citrus groves.

Vince and Audrey Cilurzo sa didn't feel they were gambling purchased the 40 acres of lan They had a weather study done and found the climate was a b Valley's. They planted their 1968 and for the next 10 yea involved in both growing and themselves. They both also classes at UC Davis and no about growing of grapes bu wine itself.

After 10 years in the bu year-old Cilurzo still consi winemaker? Her husband presently involved in bus Angeles, and she's taken angle, conducting tours part of the business.

She is pleased that V Vinnie and Chenin will the business. On weeke

See WINE/ B-2

Newspaper article about women in the wine industry in Temecula.

Phil Baily stand next to the oak aging barrels at the tasting room on Pauba Road known for library reds.

Exterior of Baily Winery.

10

Wiens Family Cellars

In 1997, grapes were first grown in the Wiens Family vineyards in Northern California near Lodi. Since most of the family lived in Southern California, the acreages in Northern California was sold and the family purchased ten acres in Temecula that had been originally planted by Brookside Winery.

Construction started on the main Temecula facility in 2005, and a temporary tasting room was opened in December of 2006. By summer of 2007, the first bride and groom held the wedding at Wiens Family Cellars.

Wiens Family Cellars provides a feeling that visitors are a member of the family. Three generations work daily at the winery and endeavor to make all visitors feel like they are members of the Wiens family. The ambiance of the winery and surrounding vineyard is the perfect setting for a wedding, large family gatherings, or corporate events, which can be held in the elegant banquet room.

Winemaker Doug Wiens is a Southern California native. He studied horticulture and business administration. His mission for the family winery is, "To make the highest quality wine and provide it at a reasonable price." The winery seal contains the words, "quality, family and integrity." These are the key mottos for the Wiens Winery. Many of the wines have been award winners.

The sign in the front of the winery states "Big Reds" wines. Wiens Family Cellars produces cabernet franc, cabernet sauvignon, zinfandel, and pinot noir. Wiens also produces a chardonnay which is aged in oak barrel and half stainless-steel tanks., as well as their ever-popular amour de l'orange sparkling wine.

Wiens has a comfortably decorated bride's room that provides a place for brides to dress and relax. There is also a groom's room for the groom and his ushers to dress and relax.

Above left: In 1997 grapes were first grown in the Wiens Family vineyards in Northern California near Lodi. Since most of the family lived in Southern California, the acreage in northern California was sold and the family purchased 10 acres in Temecula that had been originally planted by Brookside winery. Construction started on the main Temecula facility in 2003 and it opened at Christmas time of 2005. By summer of 2006 the first bride and groom held their wedding at Wiens Winery.

Above right: Grapes ripening on the vine.

The vineyard at Wiens Family Cellars.

Left: The Wiens Vineyards.

Below: Wiens Winery is known for their selection of Big Red Wines.

Christmas in the tasting room at Wiens Family Cellars.

Christmastime at Wiens Family Cellars.

This is an aerial view of the vineyard and vast facilities at Wiens Family Cellars.

The Wiens Family Crest. Wiens produces about 23,000 cases of wine each year.

Right: The barrel room. Wiens Family Cellars produces an average of 350-400 tons of wine a year.

Below: The wine rests in American Oak Barrels. Wiens has over 500 barrels in their three barrels rooms.

One of the unique wines produced is Amour de L'Orange, which is a Champagne with a fun fruity twist.

Mary Beth Wiens Tichenor hosting the popular Wiens Book Society wine club.

Doug's sister, Beth Wiens Tichenor, conveys the fun and hospitality of the winery by hosting the winery's book club. Since 2013, the book club members have read books including some by local authors. Then, every other month, Beth hosts a dinner and discussion, with the author as an invited guest, if possible. And for an added fun aspect to the evening, the menu and wine for each book club dinner is chosen from what was featured in the book that the group has just finished reading.

Wiens Family Cellars is in the heart of the Temecula Wine Country. It includes a tasting room, events pavilion, and two outdoor patios. There is also a large state-of-the-art production facility. The winery also has an elite Reserve Cellar Room, with rich dark wood dining tables and comfy leather chairs for seated tastings. This exclusive private tasting room is available for members of the Winemakers Select Club.

VITAGLIANO VINEYARDS AND WINERY

Vitagliano Winery, one of Temecula's most beloved wineries, is located less than a mile from the hustle and bustle of the Rancho California Road winery trail. Vitagliano Winery sits as a hidden oasis ready for its guests to relax, unwind, and enjoy some of Temecula's best wines.

As they walk along classic Tuscan style cobblestone around Vitagliano's tranquil lake, guests are surrounded by lush, gorgeous landscape filled with large trees and vibrant flowers, leading to the tasting room. Guests can enjoy the exclusive wine list while sitting outside taking in the surrounding views.

Wines are crafted with love, passion, and dedication to the craft of winemaking. Owner and founder, Frank Aglio, inspired by his grandfather's love of winemaking, embarked into the wine making world with his son, Anthony. Guy Vitagliano. Frank's grandfather, and Anthony's great grandfather, was known in his native village of Santa Marina Salina, Italy, as a dynamic and passionate wine lover with a dream to bring the richness and quality of Italy's finest wines to America. Now, three generations later, that story continues, one glass at a time.

Vitagliano Winery is family owned and run by Frank and Anthony. The Vitagliano culture is to ensure guests feel at home.

Owners Frank and Lisa Aglio produce wines in the Tuscan style varietals set in a California atmosphere.

GERSHON BACUS VINTNERS

Gershon Bachus Vintners is a family owned and operated boutique winery, owned by Ken and Christina Falik. The winery opened in 2005 and was the fulfillment of a dream inspired by Ken's grandfather when he came to America from Europe in 1922. Ken's grandfather practiced the art winemaking on a small scale to be enjoyed only by family and friends. Since 2016, Gershon Bachus has also been producing varietals that adhere to Kosher Jewish law in both the manufacturing and production. The Kosher wines include: hesperus grenache, zephyrus zinfandel, erato cabernet franc, aelous estate blend, anteros estate blend, and lares mouvedre. There is no difference in the quality and taste of the finely produced Kosher wines.

Vindemia Winery

David and Gail Bradley purchased the vineyard in 2004 from Fili Ortez and Joel Rosa, who started the winery and vineyard and have been wonderful mentors. The growers have dealt with various ideas to provide the vines with the best balance, ultraviolet UV protection, and water needed to grow in the mild maritime-influenced desert conditions. Both Fili and Joel are dedicated to the passion of growing, training, and at the right moment, picking some of the best fruit in Temecula. Every bottling run, they get the first bottles to enjoy the literal fruit of their labor.

Vindemia has a European style combined with a casual Southern California atmosphere. Wine is crafted from fruit grown and harvested on the property.

Wines are produced using sustainable farming practices. Growing grapes for winemaking is a long-term procedure. Vineyards that are well-managed can have a life span of twenty-five years or more. Because of this, protecting the ecosystems in which the vineyards are situated is a high priority. Enhancing and maintaining the ecosystem's integrity keeps soils and vines healthy and produces higher-quality grapes and better wines.

Pest problems are a fact of life in vineyard management, so Vindemia, along with other sustainable winegrowers, have devised numerous methods for addressing pests using biological and cultural controls that minimize impacts to the environment.

Vindemia vineyards include the following grapes: cabernet sauvignon, petite Syrah, grenache, Syrah and zinfandel—more commonly referred to as "More Cowbell."

David Bradley commented, "Once we started down the journey of selection of rootstocks, varieties and clones, things began to change and require a deeper understanding of each step. Early on, it become clear that making high quality grapes in Temecula would require money, labor, continuing education and consultants who had already considered the challenging and stubborn terroir. To that end, we have never stopped learning and experimenting with best practices to produce the grape quality needed to make our wines."

Vindemia has incorporated a small batch style of winemaking. This sometimes involves using older style, open-top fermentation and controlled temperature experiments. The production goal is to protect the grapes minutes after being picked and control their temperature while moving the grapes to the de-stemmer.

During the growing season, the Bradleys work to protect the essence of the wine grape's phenolics, anthocyanin, thiols, and tannins, which provide aroma and flavor of a great wine.

Dylan Bradley checking the grapes for harvest. [*Courtesy of Bradley Family*]

The vineyard at Vindemia Winery. [*Courtesy of Bradley Family*]

Vindemia works to achieve the full potential of each wine varietal. Most of the barrels are French Oak combined with some concrete tanks for aging. The production of quality red wine is one of the passions of the owners of Vindemia.

The Bradley's goal is that the wine purchased by visitors are just as enjoyable at their homes, in the company of family and friend, as when they were first sampled in the wine-country atmosphere.

Winemakers David Bradley and son, Dylan, are both commercial hot air balloon pilots with a combined fifty-seven years of experience. The winery began with the purchase of a vineyard site in Temecula and David buying barrels from Canton Cooperage after winning the Kentucky Derby Balloon Classic in Louisville.

The winery has a tranquil outdoor tasting room, which is surrounded by lush greenery overlooking the winery's five-acre vineyard and the picturesque valley. It is a tranquil relief frp, the hustle of everyday busy city jobs and living.

The outdoor tasting room at Vindemia. [*Courtesy of Bradley Family*]

14

CHAPIN FAMILY VINEYARDS

The Vineyard portion of Chapin Family Vineyards, LLC, was established in 2002 with the planting of two acres of Syrah, two-and-a-half acres of cabernet sauvignon, less than a half-acre of petit Verdot, and mourvedre grape varietals. Additional viognier, two acres of aglianico, and one acre of montepulciano grape varietals were planted in 2007. In 2016, one-and-a-fourth acres of cabernet franc was planted. Wine production began with the 2004 vintage of cabernet sauvignon, of which 200 cases were produced and released in 2006. In 2014, Rock Creek Vineyard was added. In the early years, most of the grape harvest was sold to local wineries in Temecula. Each year after 2004, the wine production increased and wine grape sales to other wineries decreased. As of 2012, 100% of the harvested grapes went into wine production for the Chapin Family Vineyards.

In July of 2011, after almost three years of engineering studies and approvals from Riverside County, a temporary wine serving area was established in the barrel room. The temporary serving area provided time for the remodeling of the former residence into a formal wine tasting bar. The new wine tasting bar and expansive patio area was officially opened in January of 2012. Since 2006, Chapin Family Vineyards, LLC, has increased production from 500 cases a year to nearly 3,000 cases per year, with a planned growth to approximately 5,000 cases.

Chapin Family Vineyards is known for the quality of their wines, service, knowledgeable wine staff, and great ambiance of the tasting room and expansive patio area. Their wine club continues to grow and has nearly doubled every year since its inception in 2008. Their wine club events are known for the wine, food, and entertainment venues. The goals of Chapin Family Vineyards are ambitious however by maintaining the wine quality and service, they are confident those goals will be achieved.

Steve Chapin is the owner and winemaker, a native of Southern California. Steve has a background in microbiology and zoology and served a tour of duty in the Navy. Steve decided to plant a vineyard on the property that he had owned for many years, located in the prime winegrowing area of Temecula, California.

Steve said, "I want our winery friends to feel like they had a great time and feel welcome in the quiet ambiance of the tasting room and patio area, a mini-vacation of sorts."

Therefore, Chapin bottle of wine reads "For the Love of Friendship."

Left: The Chapin Winery.

Below: Chapin Family Vineyard truck.

Chapin Family Vineyards grounds.

Chapin family crest.

15

Don Fernando Vineyard

The Chavira family acquired the land in the late 1980s and for about ten years, nothing much was done with the empty property. Then, around the turn of the millennium, Fernando Chavira Jr. and Steve Galt, as an escape from their jobs and the traffic in Los Angeles, became regular visitors to the vineyard.

It wasn't long before the pair went on a planting spree and planted all the vegetation that is now lush and green. The planting included a row of trees bordering the streets. Starting in 2000 Fernando Jr. and Steve started to come to the vineyard most weekends and planted the trees lining the streets, the palms and cypress trees that punctuate the landscape, and the smaller bushes and plants which enjoy the shade from the now mature trees. During this time, the front 3 acres of vineyards were planted to provide some income to cover the property taxes and general expenses.

Initially as a joke, a nephew of Fernando senior gifted him a sign that read, "Don Fernando's Vineyards." Years later the name remains.

Fernando Chavira, Jr. and Steve Galt worked in the industries of education and architecture, but after ten years of only coming to the vineyard on the weekends, they decided to permanently move to the Temecula Valley. The move was to increase the acreage of the Vineyards and, ultimately, to realize their dream of opening a boutique winery.

The decision was made to plant another six and one-half acres of the vineyards, but with a different set of priorities.

The front vineyards had been laid out traditionally, because the focus was to sell grapes for income. The new vineyards were laid out with the goal of allowing people to engage more directly with them, to increase the acreage given over to vineyards and, ultimately, to realize the dream of opening a boutique winery.

The design for Don Fernando Vineyard was different from the majority or the larger wineries in the Temecula Valley. The design incorporated the creation of "crop circles" and curving paths through the vineyards to accommodate family gatherings/weddings or larger public events, so people can be together but also wander on their own if desired. They are unique spaces, especially around sunset, to enjoy the views, the soft light, and the breezes.

The five to ten-year plan for the vineyard includes creating a small boutique winery and a bed-and-breakfast inn. The winery is planned on the on the hill edge of the flat land between the two vineyards—the design challenge will be to build a winery that bridges the unique styles of the two vineyards and designing the structure to be sitting "in" the hill—not just "on" the hill.

Don Fernando Vineyard is in a rustic country setting surrounded by nature. [*Courtesy of Steve Galt*]

Visitors enjoying vineyard at Don Fernando are treated to a day in the county with no city noise and sights around. [*Courtesy of Steve Galt*]

Steve and Fernando Jr. worked to plant and manicure the grounds and change the direction and goals of the vineyard. [*Courtesy of Steve Galt*]

The acres of the vineyard have been in the Chavira family since the late 1980s, but only recently began to take shape. [*Courtesy of Steve Galt*]

In Spanish, the word *Don* means 'the boss'. Over the years, many people have come onto the property asking to speak to Don, assuming it is a first name. [*Courtesy of Steve Galt*]

Family and friends gather to enjoy wine in the tranquil vineyard setting. [*Courtesy of Steve Galt*]

Family and friends enjoy relaxing in the shade after laboring in the vineyard. [*Courtesy of Steve Galt*]

Steve Galt said, "We don't want a circus—we want a smaller scale place in contrast to the many 'corporate feel' wineries in Temecula, where guests can quietly enjoy being surrounded by the vineyards."

The initial step towards their goal involves creating a retreat amid the vineyard with B&B accommodations in a touring coach called "Winestream" and Airstream BnB. These unique accommodations will enable visitors to be fully surrounded by the vineyard.

This space provides a meditative space for visitor that is full of character and individuality. This distinctive approach sets Don Fernando Vineyard apart from the other wineries and hotels in the Temecula area. This unique retreat will create a memorable experience for future visitors. When construction is in place for a permanent structure, the plans include keeping the "Winestream" as a fun addition. Plans being considered include moving the Winestream to different locations on the vineyard. Steve said, "always keeping in mind that people who wander may need a break and a refill!!'

Fernando Chavira Jr. and Steve Galt invited Cal Poly Pomona Architectural school and California State College Long Beach Interior design departments to use the Vineyard space for design studio projects. The Cal Poly Pomona students designed a winery for the space between the two vineyards. The Cal State Long Beach students based their design project around winetasting from several Airstreams trailers arranged throughout the property.

This is a spot in the middle of the vineyard that Steve and Fernando Jr. created so that visitors can relax and enjoy a glass of wine. [*Courtesy of Steve Galt*]

The unique tranquil resting places in Don Fernando's vineyard provide guests with a place to enjoy a glass of wine while gazing at the vineyard. [*Courtesy of Steve Galt*]

16

FOOT PATH WINERY

As a new widow, Christine searched for a new future and investment opportunities. Her search lead to purchasing a vineyard in Temecula. With the help of a real estate agent she located a property that was for sale in the valley.

The property had grapefruit and very established greenery. The parcel was twenty acres and had mature grapefruit, figs, pomegranates, tangelos, and tangerines, as well as some table grapes, red flame, and concord—however, there were no wine grapes. The land also had a house with a pool, a barn, and a double wide.

Events began to fall into place and move fast. Meanwhile, Christine made time for romance and also a new marriage.

2000 was a busy year for Christine. Her wedding was set for March 3, the move-in date for the vineyard was February 20, and adding to the complexity, she was also scheduled to start a new job on March 10. Fortunately, everything fell into place within the time frame.

Deane, Christine's husband, was able to locate organic stores that were willing to sell the fruit that was growing on the property that was purchased. In 2002, Foot Path received certification as an organic farm.

Christine meet someone who suggested planting zinfandel grape vines. It wasn't long before grape vines were purchased. Christine and Deane planted zinfandel, merlot, pinot noir, cabernet, cabernet franc, and Muscat blanc. Meanwhile, Deane was able to meet some local winemakers and got pointers on how to create a vineyard.

In 2003, they planted an area of the vineyard with more cabernet franc, Syrah, merlot, and cabernet. That same year, they joined an amateur winemakers' group in Temecula. Deane got a job working for Robert Ponte. He was able to get zinfandel grapes from Ponte if he picked them himself. The grapes that he harvested were at 31 brix and had trouble starting to ferment. Brix (bx) is a way to measure the potential alcohol content of a wine before it's made by determining the sugar level in grapes. Each gram of sugar that's fermented will turn into about one-half gram of alcohol. The fermenting grapes gave a beautiful aroma to the barn where the wine is made. The zinfandel stopped fermenting at 35 brix. Deane divided the grapes in half. Part went to a late harvest and the other half was fortified with grape alcohol.

The couple was not sure how much grape alcohol to add and found the right answer by using the Pearson's Square formula. This method provides a way to calculate the desired alcoholic strength and sugar concentration in wine.

Above left: An Oak Barrel at Foot Path Winery [*Courtesy of Christine Foote*]

Above right: Christine and Deane Foote, owners of one of the smallest wineries in Temecula. [Courtesy of Christine Foote]

The winery guards. [*Courtesy of Christine Foote*]

The port and late harvest zinfandel were entered into various contests and every time either received Gold or Silver medals. Christine and Deane were pleased at how well their wines were received and decided to plant more grapes. It wasn't long before they ordered 300 cabernet, 300 malbec, 300 petit verdot, 400 zinfandel, 400 merlot and 300 cabernet franc from a firm that were involved in the UC Davis program. The University's Department of Viticulture and Enology offers a wine executive Program. This program teaches the latest research, technologies, and business trends that effect the wine industry at present and into the future.

Christine and Deane had few stumbling blocks with permits by people who didn't seem to understand the wine business. They experienced some additional costs that were not expected, but eventually everything worked out.

Foot Path Vineyard is the only California Certified Organic Farm (CCOF) in the Temecula Valley. CCOF is a designation from the United States Department of Agriculture. Unfortunately, some of the grape vines were lost to pierce disease but replanting new vines has continued. Foot Path is a full-time job for both Christine and Deane. Seasonal organic fruit are for sale in the winery. Other than cleaning the groves and pruning, the couple does all the work on the winery themselves.

Christine said, "We have met quite a few certified wonderful people coming to taste wine here. That's what makes it fun and some have become our good friends. That is when I come from the house with a tray full of veggies, hummus, cheeses, crackers and salami. You know you are at the right place because you are part of the inner-circle and it doesn't cost you but to enjoy the pleasure of good people."

Deane Foote in the Barrel Room at Foot Path. [*Courtesy of Christine Foote*]

The family cat hides in the grape vines. [*Courtesy of Christine Foote*]

Christine and friends enjoying grapes at Foot Path Winery. Christine said, "We have met quite a few certified wonderful people coming to taste wine here. That's what makes it fun and some have become our good friends. That is when I come from the house with a tray full of veggies, hummus, cheeses, crackers, and salami. You know you are at the right place, because you are part of the inner circle and it doesn't cost you but to enjoy the pleasure of good people." [*Courtesy of Christine Foote*]

Bibliography

"History of Temecula" City of Temecula website, https://temeculaca.gov/148/History

"Celebrating 50 Years" Temecula Valley Winegrowers Association website, https://www.temeculawines.org/50-years/index.php

"Celebrating a California Ranching Legacy: Walter L. Vail," May 9, 2018 by Stephanie Herrera, California Ranchland Trust website, https://www.rangelandtrust.org/celebrating-california-ranching-legacy-walter-l-vail/

Temecula Valley Museum, Permanent Exhibits, Temecula History, http://www.temeculavalleymuseum.org/exhibitions/permanent-exhibits/

Earl Stanley Garner Exhibit Temecula Valley Museum, Permanent Exhibits, Temecula History, http://www.temeculavalleymuseum.org/exhibitions/permanent-exhibits/

Blog: The History of Temecula Valley Wine Country, December 18th, 2015, Copy courtesy of The City of Temecula and Robert Renzoni Vineyards, Courtesy Temecula Valley Wine Growers Association, https://www.temeculawines.org/blog/the-history-of-temecula-valley-wine-country/

Temecula Valley Museum, Permanent Exhibits, Temecula History, http://www.temeculavalleymuseum.org/exhibitions/permanent-exhibits/

History & Outreach, Temecula Valley Balloon Festival, https://www.tvbwf.com/about-us/history-outreach/

About Temecula Wines" Visit Temecula Valley, https://www.visittemeculavalley.com/wine/about-temecula-wines/

"Akash Winery" information provided by Sharon Cannon from Akash Winery sharon@akashwinery.com

"Palumbo Family Winery History" provided by Cindy Palumbo

"Andrews Family Biography" Oak Mountain Winery provided by Valerie Andrews

"Carter History Backgrounder," (South Coast Winery) February 2019 provided by Kristi Turek, Marguarite Clark Public Relations, Orange County, California

"Wilson Creek Winery History" provided from an interview with Mick Wilson

Baily Vineyard & Winery and Baily Estate Tasting Room information provided from an interview and information sheets from Phil Baily and from the Baily Winery Family Scrapbook

Wiens Family Cellars, information by Mary Beth Wiens Tichenor of Wiens Family Cellars

Vitagiliano Vineyard & Estate Winery, information provided by Anthony Aglio

Vice President Lake Oak Meadows & Vitagiliano Vineyards & Winery

"History of Vindemia Winery" provide by Katie Zuber, Vindemia Wine Club Manager

"History of Chapin Family Vineyards" provided by Doreen Uricchio, Marketing Manager, Chapin Family Vineyards

"History of Don Fernando Vineyard" provided by Steve Galt, associate at Don Fernando Vineyards and Nursery

"Foot Path Winery" information provided by Deane And Christine Foote